MEMORIES OF SHREWSBURY

ALTON DOUGLAS
DENNIS MOORE
ADDITIONAL RESEARCH BY
JO DOUGLAS

© 1987, ALTON DOUGLAS, DENNIS MOORE, JO DOUGLAS.
ISBN 0 947865 02 0

Published by Beacon Broadcasting Ltd., P.O. Box 303, Wolverhampton WV6 0DQ.
Printed by Windmill Printing, Portersfield Road, Cradley Heath, Warley, West Midlands. B64 7BX

CONTENTS

INDEPENDENT RADIO FOR THE WEST MIDLANDS & BLACK COUNTRY

303 metres & 990 kHz medium wave
97.2 MHz VHF/FM stereo

Beacon Broadcasting Limited PO Box 303 Wolverhampton WV6 0DQ Telephone: (0902) 757211 Telex: 336919

Dear Nostalgic,

Well, it was inevitable that I should eventually be involved in a book about Shrewsbury. My paternal grandmother, Lucy Crutchley, was born in the heart of the town at 4, Butcher Row, grandfather Thomas at 45, Old Coleham, and my father, Sidney Neville Price, at Moveage Cottages in Ellesmere Road. So, with that kind of background, when Beacon Radio announced that they were extending their services into Shropshire, I seized the opportunity to commemorate the event by delving into the marvellous heritage of photographs around, finally producing, with the aid of Dennis Moore and my wife Jo, the book you're now holding.

Without the initial enthusiasm and kindness of County Librarian Anthony Crowe we should have been hard-pressed to achieve lift-off, so our thanks go to him. Also to Local Studies Librarian Tony Carr and his colleagues for the extreme patience and good-humour they have shown towards us in our often irritating cross-researching, questioning, interrogating—call it what you will!

I should like part of this book to stand as a tribute to that remarkable man, Joseph Della Porta, who, all those years ago, (1888 to be precise) went around the town capturing, for you to relish, a record of so many of the shops and businesses.

Arm yourself with a magnifying glass and a spare hour or two and pore over the pages. Great pleasure can be had from suddenly discovering a character, a poster, or just a little something tucked away that would otherwise have been missed. As I've said before, in relation to all our other books, this is not an involved "history" book (although we do try to get our facts and figures right!) but rather a collection of images intended purely to entertain you.

I hope that you enjoy our efforts, and those of Beacon Radio, through the years to come.

Yours in friendship,

Alton

ALTON DOUGLAS is probably best known as the quizmaster (and co-writer), for three years, of the top-rated BBC Midlands TV series "Know Your Place", but he is also an after-dinner speaker, author, TV and radio character actor, ex-professional comedian, showbiz/jazz book and record reviewer, TV and radio commercial voice-over artist, one-time 5th Royal Inniskilling Dragoon Guards trombonist, the voice behind several cartoons and children's toys, etc.

He has appeared in virtually every major theatre in the U.K. (including the London Palladium) and is the veteran of hundreds of television studio warm-ups, but these days specialises in good class hotel, restaurant and conference work, as a sophisticated and highly humourous after-dinner speaker.

He has been featured as an actor in the TV programmes "Angels", "Seconds Out", "Crossroads", "A Soft Touch" and "Muck and Brass". His other television appearances include "The Golden Shot" (which he hosted on one memorable occasion), "The Knockers", "The Original Alton Douglas", "Nights at the Swan" and "Watch This Space". In 1985 he was featured on television in "The Barmaid's Arms", "Open University", "Property Rites", "Newshound" and "Murder of a Moderate Man". In 1986 he was seen in "Boon" and "Big Deal", recorded his first Radio 4 play "Mr. Peabody and the Beast" and commenced his third series of Wednesday big band programmes for Beacon Radio.

Since 1981 Alton has had the following books published:

"Memories of Birmingham"	"The Black Country at War"
"Birmingham at War Vol 1"	"Memories of the Black Country"
"Birmingham at War Vol 2"	"Joe Russell's Smethwick"
"Coventry at War"	"Alton Douglas's Know Your Place"
"Alton Douglas's Celebrity Recipes"	

November 1987 sees the publication of his 11th book "Memories of Coventry". He also has three books of nonsense verses and a collection of short stories lined up for publication.

INTRODUCTION

Shrewsbury, an old market town serving an agricultural county, has a history going back to the ninth century. It grew up on a site ideal for defence, enclosed within a horseshoe bend of the River Severn. The castle, started about 1070, was built at the neck of the river loop.

The antiquary John Leland was of the opinion that the destruction of Wroxeter (the Roman Uriconium) by the Saxon invaders was the likely cause of the foundation of Shrewsbury. Wroxeter's Britons escaped from the fierce, heathen foreigners and sought a place of refuge higher up the Severn. Sheltered within that river's loops at "the hill or head of Alders" they founded Amywddig or Pengwern, both ancient British titles for Shrewsbury. It was the Saxons who eventually gave the name Scrobbesbyrig, signifying a bury or fence overgrown with shrubs.

An alternative to Scrobbesbyrig was Salopesberia, from which came Salop as the county name and Salopian for a native of the town. The pronunciation of Shrewsbury is presumably a survival of "Shrosebury" and "Shrowesbury", as seen on a map of 1610, when spelling was phonetic.

At some time during the reign of Edward the Confessor (1042 - 1066), Shrewsbury contained 252 houses with a burgess residing in each one and contributing an annual rental of £7.16s. 6d. (£7.82½p), yielding under £2,000 in total. In those days a widow was required to pay the King £1 for a licence to marry, whilst a spinster paid 10/- (50p). Should a house be burnt by accident without negligence, then the burgess paid the King £2 and 2/- (10p) to each of his next-door neighbours. A levy of 10/- (50p) was to be paid to the Crown on the death of every burgess dying within the royal boundary. On 24th February 1204 King John gave a third Charter to Shrewsbury granting, amongst other things, liberty to hold a fair for three days annually from the first to the third of June.

The growth of Shrewsbury can be gauged from these population figures. In Edward the Confessor's time there was a count of 1,260 inhabitants. By the 14th century there were around 3,000, and a report in 1860 gave 19,681. Thirty one years later there was a jump to 26,967 and by 1933 the figure was 32,370. More recent figures are 49,566 in 1961, and 91,600 (Shrewsbury and Atcham) by 1985.

Shrewsbury is a truly beautiful Tudor town with the spires of St. Alkmund and St. Mary, the old School buildings in Castle Gates, the castle itself, the unexpectedly attractive railway station, the shops with their black and white timbered frames, the Music Hall in the Square, dating from 1840 but inside it the remains of Vaughan's Mansion of 14th century vintage; in the Abbey Foregate, the Norman Abbey (Holy Cross Church), and the present Shrewsbury School buildings.

"The streets ascend and curve about and intersect each other with the customary irregularity of old English towns, so that it is quite impossible to go directly to any given point, or for a stranger to find his way to a place which he wishes to reach, although, by what seems a singular good fortune, the sought-for place is always offering itself when least expected. I never knew such pleasant walking as in old streets like those of Shrewsbury." So wrote Nathaniel Hawthorne, the American author (1804 - 1864). We are happy to agree with him.

BEGINNINGS

Shrewsbury School was founded by Edward VI in 1552. The school's buildings, that are now the town's Library, were erected during the period 1590 to 1630, so the real beginnings of the school were probably in Rigg's Hall, close by. The move to Kingsland was made in 1882, occupying the buildings of the Shrewsbury Foundling Hospital as it was originally in 1765. The Girls' High School, Town Walls, was in use by 1897, but boys waited until 1910 for the construction of their Priory County School for Boys.

To cater for domestic science, Radbrook College was built in Radbrook Road, having fine red brick, attractive gables and a symmetrical front.

The Technical College was built on the site of the demolished Carline's House in 1938, to become the Wakeman School as it is today.

The Youth Hostels Association (YHA) started in 1930, promoting youthful, healthy, outdoor activity combined with a sense of self-sufficiency. This was to prove most beneficial to Service recruits during the Second World War. There has been a hostel of some sort in Shrewsbury since 1934, but it was in 1939 when the present premises in Abbey Foregate were purchased, the opening of these being delayed until 1946 due to the Second World War.

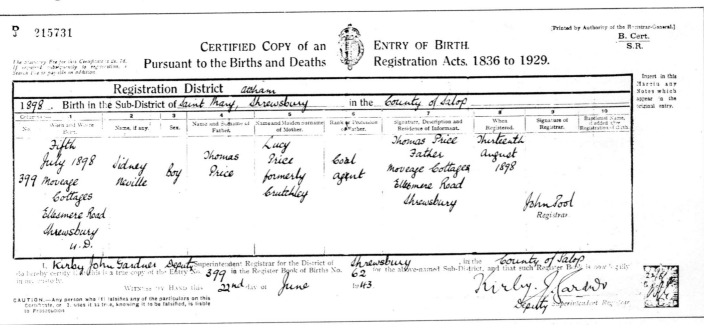

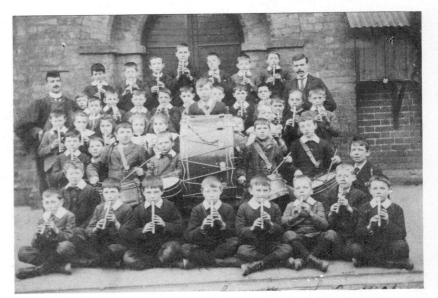

Shrewsbury Lancasterian School Band, 2nd March 1901.

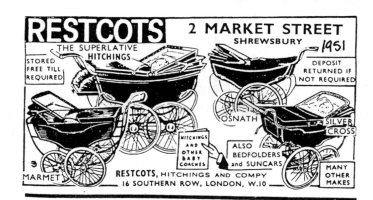

Miss E. Wallett's School, 167 Abbey Foregate, c. 1903.

Allatt's School, c. 1908.

Shrewsbury School Chapel Choir, 1922/23.

Sundorne School, 1910.

Prestfelde School, July 1933.

Coleham School Athletics Team. Winners of the Inter-School Sports, 1929/30.

St. George's School F.C., Frankwell, 1938/39.

Time Table

Cobham Junior Mixed School.

Analysis

No. of minutes in week devoted to each subject	IVa	IVb	IIIa	IIIb	IIa	IIb
English	455 / 495	455 / 495	570 / 550	575 / 545	580 / 580	477 / 565
Mathematics	225	225	225	225	225	5
History	55	60	60	55	55	60
Geography	70	60	70	60	60	60
Physical Training	100	100	100	100	95	100
Nature Study	70	70	65	60	70	60
Art	70	70	70	70	70	40
Needlework	125	125	125	125	125	70
Music	55	60	55	60	60	55
Handwork	55	55	55	55	55	55
Religious Inst.	150	150	150	150	150	150
Organised Games	55	55	75	–	–	–
Registration	75	75	75	75	75	75
Total no. of Minutes	1475	1475	1475	1475	1475	1475

Special Times for Girls in English and Art shown in Red ink.

Registers are closed at 9.10 a.m. and 1.50 p.m. respectively.

Approved on behalf of the L.E.A.

Approved on behalf of the Board of Education
H.M.I. photos

E. Thomas H.T. 16.37

TIMETABLE
1937.

THEY ALSO SERVE

The Fire Brigade and Police Force emerged and developed from beginnings typical of other communities throughout the country: the Brigade from the control of the insurance companies and the Force from an understaffed, and therefore a weak organisation. By 1860 Shrewsbury's Police Force consisted of one head constable, two first class and one second class sergeants, one first class, nine second class and nine third class constables.

The Salvation Army, that great movement for evangelising and assisting the rougher and poorer elements of society, was founded by the Rev. William Booth in 1879. The opposition which its novel methods at first aroused was gradually overcome.

The Red Cross was formed in 1870, the St. John Ambulance in 1887 and the Women's Royal Voluntary Service (as the W.V.S.) in 1937.

An Eye, Ear and Throat Hospital was built in Murivance in 1881, opposite Allatt's School.

```
                SALOP FIRE BRIGADE

SCALE OF CHARGES FOR ATTENDING FIRES

Superintendent, First two hours or less time      0. 10. 0
                for every succeeding hour         0. 02. 0
Firemen, First hour, for each Fireman             0.  3. 0
Firemen, Second and Third hours ditto - per hour  0.  1. 6
Firemen, for every succeeding hour - ditto -      0.  1. 0
Pumpers and Assistants  Additional
For Wear and Tear of Engine and Hose
        or of Hose Reel                            1.  1. 0
Cleaning-up                                     Actual Cost
Horses and Drivers, according to distance
Refreshments, according to actual cost


                          By Order
                        of the Committee
                            1901

NO CHARGE for attending Fires for
Properties insured in the SALOP, and
SHROPSHIRE & NORTH  WALES & ALLIANCE
FIRE OFFICES
```

RIOT ACT.

The Statute 1 Geo. 1, stat. 2, c. 5, contains the proclamation known as the "Riot Act," which is to be read aloud by a magistrate, sheriff, sub-sheriff, or mayor, in the presence of the rioters, silence being first commanded. The following is the form of proclamation:—

PROCLAMATION.

(silence having been first commanded):—

"Our Sovereign Lord the King chargeth and commandeth all persons being assembled immediately to disperse themselves and peaceably to depart to their habitations or lawful business upon the pains contained in the Act made in the first year of the reign of the late King George the First for preventing tumultuous and riotous assemblies. 'God save the King.'"

The proclamation can only be read when TWELVE or MORE PERSONS are "unlawfully, riotously, and tumultuously assembled together to the disturbance of the public peace."

Salop Fire Brigade, c. 1900.

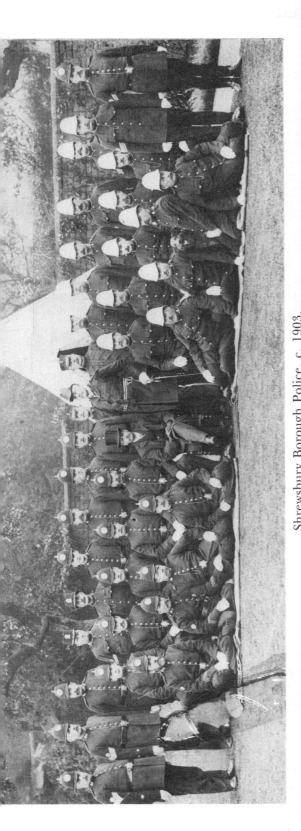

Shrewsbury Borough Police, c. 1903.

Shrewsbury Borough Police, 1922.

Shrewsbury Borough and Shropshire County Police serving in
the Guards, July 1915.

The Army in action in Longden Coleham, First World War.

Ready for fire-fighting, Cross Hill, Second World War.

Warrant Officers and Sergeants, The King's Shropshire Light Infantry, April 1935.

Army Form Z. 21.

CERTIFICATE of * { Discharge / Transfer to Reserve / Disembodiment / Demobilization } on Demobilization.

Regtl. No. 321517   Rank Fl. Cadet

Names in full Ward Cecil
(Surname first)

Unit and Regiment or Corps
from which } Royal Air Force
Discharged
Transferred to Reserve

Enlisted on the 9 October 191 5

For Royal Army Service Corps,
(Here state Regiment or Corps to which first appointed)

Also served in Royal Air Force

Only Regiments or Corps in which the Soldier served since August 4th, 1914, are to be stated. If inapplicable, this space is to be ruled through in ink and initialled.

† Medals and
Decorations } Pending verification
awarded during
present engagement

*Has
Has not } served Overseas on Active Service.

Place of Rejoining in
case of emergency } Shrewsbury   Medical Category A I

Specialist Military
Qualifications } Pilot Lms   Year of birth 1894

Is this { Discharged / Transferred to Army Reserve / Disembodied / Demobilized } on 26 June 191 9

in consequence of Demobilization.

_____ Signature and Rank.

Officer i/c R.A.F. Records.

Blandford (Place).

* Strike out whichever is inapplicable.
† The word "Nil" to be inserted when necessary.

GD1525 200,000 8/18 HWV(P1014)

WARNING.—If this Certificate is lost a duplicate cannot be issued. You should therefore on no account part with it, or forward it by post when applying for a situation.

N.B.—Any person finding this Certificate is requested to forward it in an unstamped envelope to the Secretary, War Office, London, S.W.I.

Some of the voluntary workers who prepared the Armoury as a
Hostel for Belgian Refugees, London Road, 1917.

British Red Cross "Presentation of Colours" Parade enters
The Square, 25th July 1954.

Royal Salop Infirmary, July 1914.

18

St. John Ambulance and V.A.D. Nurses, St. John Auxiliary Military Hospital, Oakley Manor, 1914/1919.

Dedication of Girl Guides County Standard, St. Mary's, 1951. Lady Baden-Powell, Chief Guide, greets a Standard Bearer, whilst Mrs. Thole, the County Commissioner, looks on.

W.V.S. (now W.R.V.S.) 21st Birthday Expedition about to set off for Coventry and Warwick Castle, 3rd June 1959.

The 26th Shrewsbury Scout Group at their H.Q., Field Crescent, 1956.
The Group was formed in 1937.

IN TOWN

The small, compact area we call the town centre measures about a quarter of a square mile and within that section we find such quaint names as Dogpole, Grope Lane, Pride Hill, Shoplatch, Wyle Cop, Murivance and Town Walls. Butcher Row, Fish Street, Milk Street and Laundry Lane speak for themselves.

Charles I and Prince Rupert stayed for a time in Shrewsbury, having captured the town in 1645, and Mary Tudor resided for a while in a house in Dogpole. Henry VII stayed at Henry Tudor House on his way to Bosworth Field in 1485; Charles Dickens was a guest at the Lion Hotel in Wyle Cop for a time.

The Shrewsbury Commercial and Literary Circular.

KING'S HALL CINEMA.

To-day and Saturday Maria Paudler in "The Last Fort" is being screened. It is the story of three white men who have thrown in their lot with the Arabs who are the last line in defence in Fort Abu Hassi against the onslaught of the French. The three of them are embittered woman-haters, and when a young white girl comes to the fort in quest of her missing father, the situ-

ation changes. Two of the whites scheme to possess the girl, but are continually frustrated by the finer-natured Brant. There is a wealth of dramatic incident, and the atmosphere of anti-feminine venom in which two of the three white men are steeped is most powerfully suggested in a series of vividly dramatic scenes.

Monday and Tuesday next, Dec. 23rd and 24th, popular Mabel Poulton and Clifford McLaglen in "The Alley Cat" is to be shown

St. John's Hill, c. 1890.

Hills Lane, c. 1905.

Claremont Street, 1865.

23

Mardol Head, c. 1898.

Mardol, 1938.

Pride Hill, c. 1890.

Sun Inn, Roushill, c. 1889.

25

Castle Street, September 1933.

Castle Gates/Meadow Place, 1933.

Castle Gates, 1933.

26

Station Yard, c. 1890.

Admiral Benbow's House, Coton Hill, 1890.

Fish Street, c. 1905.

Milk Street, c. 1902.

Princess Street, c. 1896.

JAMES DAVIES, Meat Purveyor,

Bacon Curer, Sausage and Pork Pie Manufacturer (Wholesale and Retail). 1906

DAVIES.

Supply of
BUTTER and
EGGS
from his Farms

SHOPS :

3 & 82 Wyle Cop,

9 & 10 Mardol . .

36 Castle Street,

SHREWSBURY.

Pickled Tongues and
Home Pressed Beef
always in Stock.

Families supplied
on reasonable terms.

Carriage paid
on goods up to
100 miles.

Only First-Class
Quality . . .
Supplied . . .

Butcher Row, c. 1890.

Butcher Row, 1st July 1893.

Butcher Row, June 1895.

Ireland's Mansion, High Street, c. 1890.

High Street, c. 1905.

High Street, 1923.

The Square, c. 1890.

The Square, c. 1910.

MADDOX:

13/5/31

FOR HOLIDAY WEAR AND ACCESSORIES

TWO SMART COATS
— moderately priced. —

SMART TAILOR MADE COAT in fine quality fancy suiting of Blue and Grey mixture, flap pockets, lined best quality Art Twill.
Price **65/6**

SUITING COAT in the new diagonal effect, stand collar and fancy cuffs. Five rows of stitching on revere and fronts, lined throughout Art Twill.
Price **3½ Gns.**

SPECIAL VALUE.

TENNIS FROCKS

in "Delysia" Art Silk, cut with full flared skirt in front, high waist line, finished with belt & buckle. Shades: White, Blue, Pink, Beige. **12/6**

S UNNY days are here, and there are many things you will require. At Maddox may be found a really beautiful selection of delightful Summer Wear—for every occasion.

NEW GREEN FIGURED NINON 2-PIECE SLEEVELESS FROCK, lined through Georgette, full skirt with new hip line, smart Coatee, suitable for every occasion, **89/6**

GREEN FIGURED ART GEORGETTE FROCK, V Neck, moulded to fit hip line, with tucks, new flounce at hip, and sleeves, lined through with Art Georgette slip **65/6**

AFTERNOON FROCK in Green and Brown printed Crepe-de-Chene, smart Collar, Cuffs and Jabot of self Green embroidered with silk to tone, new hip flounce, fashionable length. **52/6**

TRAVEL REQUISITES, etc.

MOROCCO GRAIN FIBRE SUIT CASE, metal bound edges, protected corners, Klipit Locks. A most attractive light case. 24in. **6/11**

LADIES' EXPANDING FIBRE CASE, Willow cloth finish, delightful shade of wine. 22in. **33/6**

NUT COWHIDE SUIT CASE, fibre foundation, cloth lined, metal frame, solid Brass locks, exceptional value. 24 x 14½ x 6¼. PRICE **28/6**

SOFT TOP BLOUSE CASES, lined, attractively printed cotton, various colours. 16in. **7/11**

HAT CASES TO MATCH **5/11**

SIX HOOP CABIN TRUNK, 3 ply Birchwood foundation, covered Brown painted canvas, metal corners, and hoops metal protected on corners, sliding nozel locks, centre clip. 36in. **36/6**

HARLEQUIN PICNIC CASES, brown fibre cases, with washable lining, containing Thermos Flask, semi porcelain cups and saucers, sandwich tins, cutlery, etc., for —
2 persons, **16/9**
4 persons **22/6**

MAKE YOUR GARDEN A PLACE OF DELIGHT this Whitsuntide !

DECK CHAIR, Strong Frame, Good Quality Canvas **3/6**

DECK CHAIR, Full Size, Striped Canvas **3/11**

DECK CHAIR, Full Size, Stronger Frame and Canvas **4/9**

FOLDING ARM CHAIR, Canvas Seat and Back ... **8/9**

FOLDING ARM CHAIR, Canvas Seat and Back, complete with tray and awning **21/-**

SELF-ADJUSTING DECK CHAIR, very comfortable **10/6**

STRONG, FOLDING GARDEN SHELTERS, with striped or plain Canvas .... **25/- 39/6 45/-** each.

GARDEN SWING LOUNGE, with spring seat, adjustable awning .... **£6/19/6** each.

AN INVITATION

To practical Lectures and Demonstrations, which will be given on the following days:
Monday, Tuesday, Wednesday, Friday and Saturday, at 11 a.m. and 3 p.m.
Thursday ... ... at 11 a.m.

by Miss A. RICH,
WELDON'S LONDON EXPERT,

on "Home Dressmaking".

Maddox
Shrewsbury's Senior Store

R. MADDOX & CO., LTD., HIGH STREET AND PRIDE HILL, SHREWSBURY.

Miscellaneous Advertisements 1951

GRAMOPHONE RECORDS: Shropshire's largest and most up-to-date stock is now at Wildings of Shrewsbury.

BOOK, RECORD, PICTURE and GIFT TOKENS: They all make ideal presents from 5/- upwards and can be obtained personally or by post from Wilding & Son Limited, Castle Street, Shrewsbury.

A LARGE SELECTION of French Corduroy Velvets, by Rumonté, in Coats, Suits, Jackets and Cardigans can always be seen at Salop Furriers, 5 High Street, Shrewsbury.

FOUNTAIN PEN REPAIRS carried out by experts.—Wilding & Son Ltd., Castle St., Shrewsbury.

GRAMOPHONE REPAIRS carried out by skilled mechanic. — Wildings of Shrewsbury

BOOKS BY POST: We specialise in selling Books by Post and from our Bookshop we send parcels to all parts of the World. So, whenever you want a Book, write to Wildings of Shrewsbury.

PICTURE FRAMING: We have our own Framing Workshops and shall be happy to help you in your choice of suitable mouldings for any of your own prints or photographs. We always have a large stock of framed Pictures and Prints by well-known artists and they make ideal presents at all times.— Wildings of Shrewsbury.

A PRESENT from Wildings' Gift Shop reflects the highest standard of good taste. We have many delightful gifts that carry little or no purchase tax and you can, therefore, still obtain from us those Wedding and other Gifts for special occasions at a price you want to pay.—Wilding & Son Ltd., Castle Street, Shrewsbury.

YOUR TYPEWRITING should be done by The Duplicating Bureau, Harlescott, Shrewsbury. Telephone 2117.

PEDIGREE IRISH SETTERS, born March 2nd—Outstanding puppies. 6 guineas.— White Cottage, Codsall. 'Phone 344 (evenings).

ABOVE SURRENDER VALUE paid for Endowment policies. "Pearl" weeklies bought.—Hiscock-Keeping (Sm), Heath Road, Twickenham.

MORTGAGES. Entire purchase price and costs advanced to tenant purchasers. 90% others.—Hiscock-Keeping (SM) Heath Road, Twickenham.

FOR PRINTING that is urgent try the Shrewsbury Chronicle Ltd., Printing Department, 'Phone 4444. To secretaries and organisers let us quote you for printing your Posters, Tickets, etc.

HOLIDAY Cardigans for cool evenings (hand knitted). Sweaters, etc., knitted in club colours.—Edith Watkins, Knitwear Parlour, Shrewsbury.

HAND KNITTED GARMENTS, also hand woven trolley cloths, scarves, etc.— Edith Watkins, Knitwear Parlour, 25 Talbot Chambers, Market Street, Shrewsbury.

FOOTBALL FANS ! Club colours knitted into scarves, etc. Quotations willingly supplied.—Edith Watkins, Knitwear Parlour.

Holiday Accommodation

BLACKPOOL — Nixons, 54 Tyldesley Rd. Close to Prom. and Manchester Hotel. Tel. 23629. Board 12/6 per day. July and August 13/6.

CANTERBURY Nr. Hotel Celeste, Molash, Kent. A real rest in lovely country. Southern aspect. Central heating. H. & C. Interior sprung mattresses. Home produce, excellent cooking. Homely atmosphere. Resident proprietors. Licensed. From 5 gns. Tel. Challock 330. Brochure.

EIRE FOR HOLIDAYS, Imperial Hotel, Wexford. Fully licensed. Excellent catering. Terms moderate.

LLANDUDNO. Enola Guest House, Church Walks. Telephone 7116. Highly recommended. Mrs. Soubrand.

LLANDUDNO -- Woodlee Private Hotel. Adjacent West Parade. Near Tennis and Golf. Home - made cakes, pastries, etc. Vi-Spring beds, H. and C. all bedrooms. Five to Seven Guineas weekly according to season. Telephone 732311.

ST. ANNES-ON-SEA—Sunningdale Hotel, 11 South Prom. Facing pier. Homely, Prop. A. Rowley. 'Phone 2053.

SEAFORD, SUSSEX. Burdyke Private Hotel. Adjacent sea and unspoilt country-side, offers quietness, finest cuisine and all the amenities of the South Coast.—Write or 'Phone 2977.

SOUTHSEA — "Homelea," 22 Worthing Road. H. and C. Slumberlands. Lounge. Board from 3½ guineas. Early or late.— 'Phone 5923.

SNOWDONIA NATIONAL PARK. Bryn Celyn Private Hotel, Llanfairfechan, (A.A. approved) affords an ideal centre and is extremely comfortable and beautifully situated overlooking the sea. Brochure with pleasure. Telephone 97.

WESTON - SUPER - MARE — Homely Board Residence. Recommended.—Mrs. Butters, 11 Upper Bristol Road.

WESTON-SUPER-MARE. Luxury four-berth Caravans to let at Uphill. Flush sanitation. Calor gas oven stoves and lighting. Sept. 5 guineas weekly.—F. Wallis, 16 Martins Road, Hanham, Bristol.

SPRING BACK BINDERS

suitably lettered The Shropshire Magazine providing quick and permanent binding up to twelve issues.

See page 14

Frankwell, c. 1895.

String of Horses, Frankwell, c. 1904.

Frankwell, c. 1905.

Frankwell, 1908.

37

ON THE MOVE

The narrowness and steepness of Shrewsbury's highways made them unsuitable for trams or trolley-buses. Passengers of an earlier time used the horse or horse-drawn vehicles.

Various forms of craft were used on the river. The Severn coracle goes back possibly 4,000 years. This boat, made to carry one person, was rounded and basin-like, and had a frame of ash laths covered with a skin of tarred canvas. It was paddled or sculled and, as well as being a fishing-craft, would also have been used to travel from one bank to the other in the nature of a ferry.

The Victorians were great lovers of the open air and formed cycling clubs. The railway arrived in Shrewsbury in 1848, providing essential, swift transport for produce and people, but in the early days, before the advent of fail-safe signalling and adequate track maintenance, numerous accidents occurred.

Coach of A.C. McCorquodale of Cound, High Sheriff of Salop, at St. Chad's Church, 1912.

Laundry Lane, c. 1912.

A Sentinel Bus,

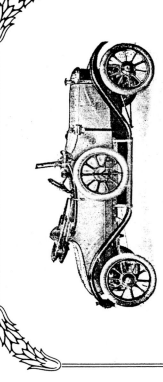

No. 73026 approaching Sutton Bridge junction, c. 1952.

"Lord Kitchener", c. 1954.

No. 42400 at Shrewsbury Station, c. 1954.

"Duke of Gloucester", c. 1955.

AT WORK

The fact that various markets have been held on a number of sites for over 1,000 years is evidence of Shrewsbury's status as a truly market town. Local cakes, brawn, ale and cheese become renowned and helped considerably in satisfying the needs of visitors, tourism being another of the town's industries.

As an important road and railway centre, the town gave birth to major industries, for example the Midland Railway Carriage Works at Coleham.

Boat building and fishing-tackle trades flourished along the river-banks and there were river cruises.

The Sentinel Waggon Works in Whitchurch Road, built steam waggons, diesel tractors, gas-engines and buses.

A most notorious factory was Burr's Lead Works of the 1840's which disgorged waste so lethal that animals and humans alike succumbed in large numbers at nearby Coleham. Timber merchants, saw-mills and cabinet makers carried on trade along Smithfield Road, aided by the proximity of the river and its wharves.

Safe-making, tools and dies all have their place in Shrewsbury's industrial scene.

Midland Railway Carriage Works, Coleham, c. 1893.

Office Staff, Midland Railway Carriage Works, Abbey Foregate, c. 1886.

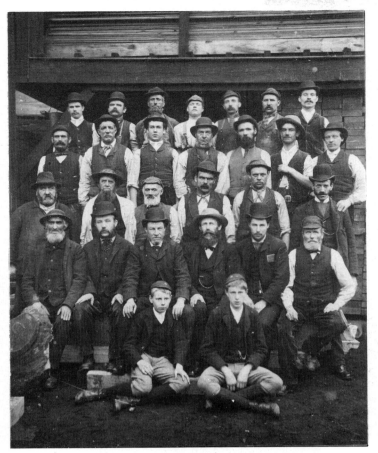

Barker Bros., Smithfield Road, 1888.

William Wilson, Smithfield Road Steam Saw Mills, c. 1890.

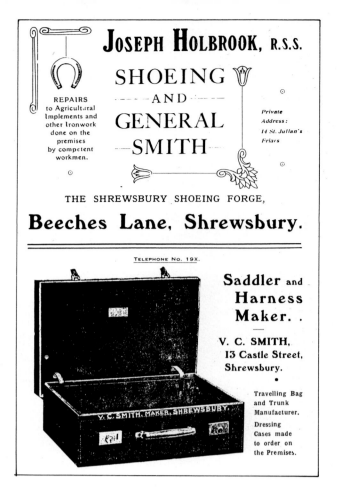
Walker's Printing Offices, Fish Street, c. 1910.

Royal Show Staff, 1914.

Corbet's Perseverance Ironworks, Castle Foregate, 1888.

Sentinel stand at the exhibition in the Working Men's Hall,
23rd - 28th February 1948.

Sentinel Waggon Works, c. 1928.

Legge & Co., c. 1928.

Roadwork in Smithfield Road, 1932.

The temporary bridge in operation.
English Bridge, September 1925.

48

Smithfield, Raven Meadows, c. 1896.

Cheeses for sale, General Market, c. 1932.

Last auction, Smithfield, 1959.

AT PLAY

Football has always been popular in Shrewsbury since as early as the 16th Century. In 1563, two men were imprisoned locally for fighting whilst playing on All Saints' Day. Shrewsbury F.C. was established in 1886, playing at the racecourse and utilising "volunteers". Full professional players were employed in the 1920's but even in 1936 a mere £40 per week was the total wages bill. The present ground, the Gay Meadow, was leased from the Corporation in 1910 and purchased in 1960.

The first known rowing club in Shropshire was Shrewsbury's Pengwern Boating Club, of 1835, known as the Blue Club because of the members' blue jackets. It was disbanded in 1849. Shrewsbury School took a keen interest in the sport and helped to promote it locally, holding regattas from 1854.

Cock-fighting, known to have taken place at the town gaoler's house in 1598, was supported by the local gentry, but had lost its popularity with them by the middle of the last century.

Fishing has long been popular, often with the use of Severn coracles, and salmon poaching became common. The Shrewsbury Angling Association was inaugurated in 1879.

Hare-coursing was fashionable on the Corbet Estate, Sundorne, in the mid-19th century. The True Blue fox hunters of 1753 became the Shrewsbury Hunt in 1769, later becoming the Shrewsbury Hunt Club.

Horse racing at Kingsland in 1718 ended in 1724 but revived in 1729 when a new course was used at Bicton Heath.

Locally, the Cricket Club was formed in 1862, the Golf Club in 1890 and the Rugby Club in 1908.

St. George's F.C., 1923/4.

Shrewsbury Police Football Team, 5th May 1938.

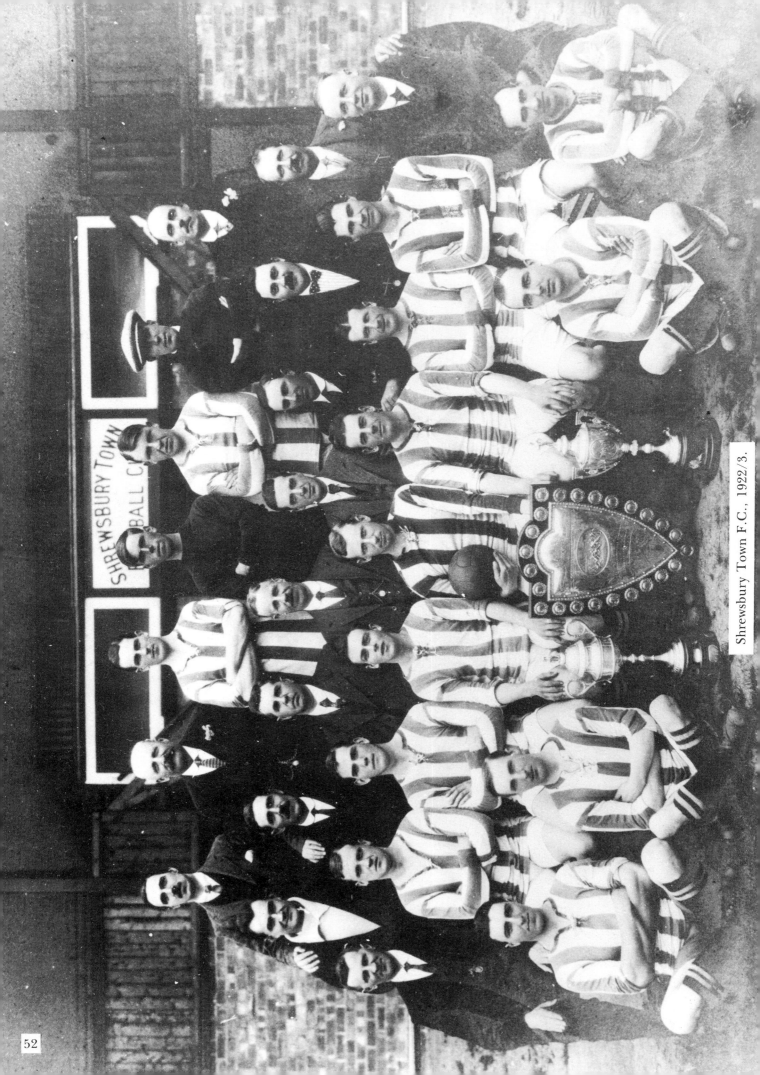

Shrewsbury Town F.C., 1922/3.

Shrewsbury Rugby Club, 1936.

Shrewsbury Cricket Club, 1936.

Eton Fives Team, Shrewsbury School, 1921/22.

Public Baths, 1910.

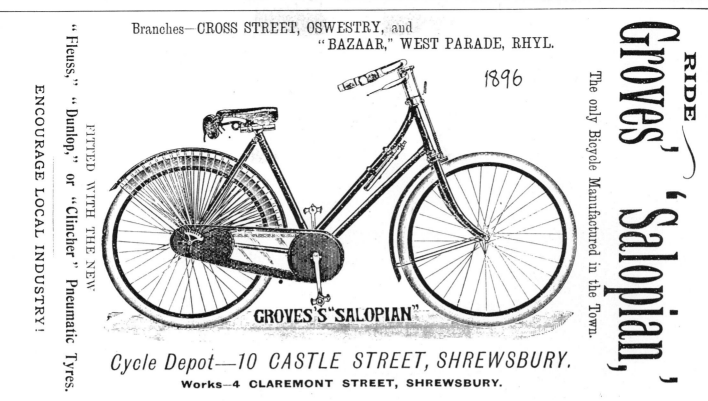
SALOP MOTOR CLUB (SHREWSBURY)

(President: J. G. FENN-WIGGIN, ESQ.)

In Conjunction With

KINGS NORTON MOTOR - CYCLE CLUB (1944)

(President: W. HOMER, ESQ.)

Both Members of Midland Centre A.C.U. Will Organise

HAWKSTONE SCRAMBLE

SUNDAY, AUGUST 17th, 1952

(A.C.U. Permit No. F.578)

Programme 6d.

—— Officials of the Meeting ——

A.C.U. Steward	Mrs. Doris Taylor
Club Stewards	S. Seston, H. Embrey
Timekeeper and Judge	J. G. Fenn-Wiggin, Esq.
Hon. Medical Officer	A. E. McCorkell, M.B.
Hon Treasurer	C. J. Statham, F.C.S.
Clerk of the Course	L. Launchbury
Chief Marshals	Ken Ward and W. Wright
Starter	W. Higgins
Chief Paddock Marshal	R. Liversage
Competitors' Marshal	J. Hopkins
Lap Scorers	F. Dorrell, S. Latham and H. Mansfield
Machine Examiners	J. Meredith and E. Minor
Programmes	Mrs. C. O. Bate
Secretary of Meeting	C. O. Bate

1. Marine Cottage, English Bridge, Shrewsbury.

Music and Announcements by Vernon Cooper Ltd., Radio House, Nantwich

Refreshments and Ices by T. Sidoli and Sons.

THE SALOP MOTOR CLUB respectfully ask you **TO BE CAREFUL AND TAKE ALL PRECAUTIONS TO PREVENT FIRE.**

Brigadier Sir Alexander Stanier, Bart., has kindly given permission for this Event to be held

EVENT 1. UNLIMITED FOR SALOP RESIDENT RIDERS. FOUR LAPS. Five Awards.		EVENT 2. MACHINES NOT EXCEEDING 250 c.c. FOUR LAPS. Five Awards.	
16.	Capt. J. R. Stephens.	3.	Les Archer.
331.	Jack Davies.	8.	Ron Cox.
317.	Ken Lock.	16.	Capt. J. R. Stephens.
30.	Brian Jackson.	20.	J. Underwood.
9.	Derek Garbett.	328.	M. Randall.
12.	Ken Davies.	158.	E. G. C. Manton.
27.	J. Hopkins.	55.	Den Bickerton.
197.	Brian Roberts.	184.	F. E. Smith.
21.	Don Williams.	71.	Tres. Sharp.
352.	W. Lewis.	70.	Bryan Sharp.
304.	Gordon Davies.	197.	Brian Roberts.
263.	Don Lawley.	263.	Don Lawley.
289.	Bern Walley.	372.	D. G. Williams.
24.	P. H. Blomer.	245.	J. Pizzey.
75.	B. F. Blomer.	323.	G. Smith.
291.	J. R. Flood.	32.	R. Probert.
15.	Trevor Garbett.	318.	J. H. Hilton.
323.	Geo. Smith.	370.	A. J. Liddiard.
32.	R. Probert.	22.	D. Tye.
14.	Gordon Boulton.		
18.	Ben Bard.		
28	Jim Gwilliam.		

• Warning – Motor Racing is Dangerous

You are present at this meeting entirely at your own risk, and tickets of admission are issued subject to the condition that all persons having any connection with the promotion and/or organisation and/or conduct of this meeting, including the owners of the land and the drivers and owners of the vehicles and passengers in the vehicles, are absolved from all liability in respect of personal injury (whether fatal or otherwise) to you or damage to your property howsoever caused.

The first scramble held at Hawkstone Park.

Theatre Royal, Shoplatch, 1931.

Railway Queen at the Music Hall, 1932.

The MUSIC HALL

SHREWSBURY. *1888*

Is the only ROOM in THE TOWN of sufficient size and convenience for

Concerts, Entertainments,

AND

PUBLIC MEETINGS.

It will hold nearly 1000 people, is brilliantly lighted, fully supplied with Seats ; has Retiring Rooms, possesses facilities for every occasion of Public Assemblies, and is considered to be in its acoustic properties, unsurpassed for Musical effect.

THE HALL IS FULLY LICENSED FOR

Stage Plays.

The Length is 90 feet; Width 42 feet; Height 38 feet. This measurement is inclusive of

A RAISED ORCHESTRA

THE FULL WIDTH OF THE HALL.

The Population of Shrewsbury is nearly 27,000.

For Terms, Vacant Dates, or any further information, apply to

V. C. L. CRUMP,

Secretary and Manager.

1922

KING'S HALL, WYLE COP, SHREWSBURY

THE MOST CINEMA UP-TO-DATE
—— IN THE MIDLANDS. ——

THE CREAM OF THE CINEMA WORLD

DRAMA, COMEDY, COMIC,

—— EDUCATIONAL, ——

HISTORICAL AND TRAVEL.

PATHÉS GAZETTE WITH THE LATEST EVENTS ALWAYS SHOWN

Continuous Performances Daily
From 2-30 to 10-15.

Popular Prices:—Private Boxes, 9/2. Balcony, 1/3. Auditorium, 8d. & 4d.
(Including Entertainment Tax).

MANAGER ... CHARLES BAYLEY.

Electric Fans. **Telephone 367.**

Cool in Summer. Warm in Winter.

Music in the Square, c. 1890.

Frankwell Prize Jazz Band, 1937.

Dance Group at Morris's Cafe Ballroom, Pride Hill, 1933.

Time for Fancy Dress at Morris's, c. 1935.

59

THE LATE TWENTIES

EVENTS

This volume is not intentionally a history book. In fact, if all of Shrewsbury's important events were reported here, there would be little space left for our photographs! However, we mention just a few.

In 1403, the bloody and cruel Battle of Shrewsbury saw the death of Henry or Harry Percy (called Hotspur) whose body (after the victory by Henry IV) was mutilated on a spot at the junction of Castle Street and Pride Hill.

In 1774 the English Bridge bore houses and was distinctly hump-backed until 1926 when it was widened and its pitch lessened.

The Welsh Bridge was in position to receive tolls as early as 1262. Early drawings show a turreted gateway which was removed in 1791 and the "new" bridge as we know it today was built in 1795.

God's wrath was said to have been vented on some of Shrewsbury's folk for their support of Charles Darwin (born in the town in 1809) with his theories on the origins of the human species, by a gale in February 1894 which toppled the spire of St. Mary's Church, wrecking the nave roof.

The unveiling of Darwin's Memorial by the Shropshire Horticultural Society. Castle Gates, 1897.

Proclamation of the Accession of George V, 1910.

Queen Mary at the Flower Show, 1927.

Civic Parade, Old Market Hall,
c. 1936.

Opening of the Waterworks at
Shelton by Viscount Bridgeman,
4th July 1935.

The Rev. W.B. MacNab feeds imprisoned cottagers in Abbey Gardens, Abbey Foregate, 23rd January 1899.

The Bus Station, 9th February 1946.

Chester Street, 1947.

Railway Disaster, 1907.

On the rails again, after the
accident, 1907.

The funeral of Leonard Bradley and Stephen
Hodgson, GPO clerks killed at Shrewsbury
Station, 18th October 1907.

Funeral of The Marquis of Cambridge (Queen Mary's brother), 26th October 1927.

Consecration of the Church of England portion of the cemetery extension by The Bishop of Lichfield, 21st October 1939.

One of the few bombs that fell on Shrewsbury during the Second World War landed on Moveage Cottages, Ellesmere Road, where Alton's father was born. The clearing up is about to start. 31st August 1940.

67

A welcome cup of hot soup served on English Bridge, 11th November 1934.

Recruiting March for The Grenadiers. Welsh Bridge, 1929.

Pride Hill, May 1937.

Coronation celebrations in Castle Street, May 1937.

THE DELLA PORTA COLLECTION

Many people will remember the Della Porta store in Shrewsbury, an enterprise geared to providing the customer with the highest possible level of courtesy and satisfaction. Joseph Lewis Della Porta, son of the founder, who took over management of the store, was a keen cyclist and photographer. He was among the first in the town to ride a pennyfarthing, on which he cycled to London and later toured France.

In 1888, when aged 25, he produced a fine collection of photographs. This section is composed of some of them.

Joseph died on 7th July 1929. The store was acquired by Rackhams in 1976.

Morgan & Son, 2 Market Street.

5 Market Street.

4 Mardol Head.

7 Mardol Head.

NAPIER. STATIONER PRINTER

BOOK, STATIONERY & FANCY GOODS DEPÔT

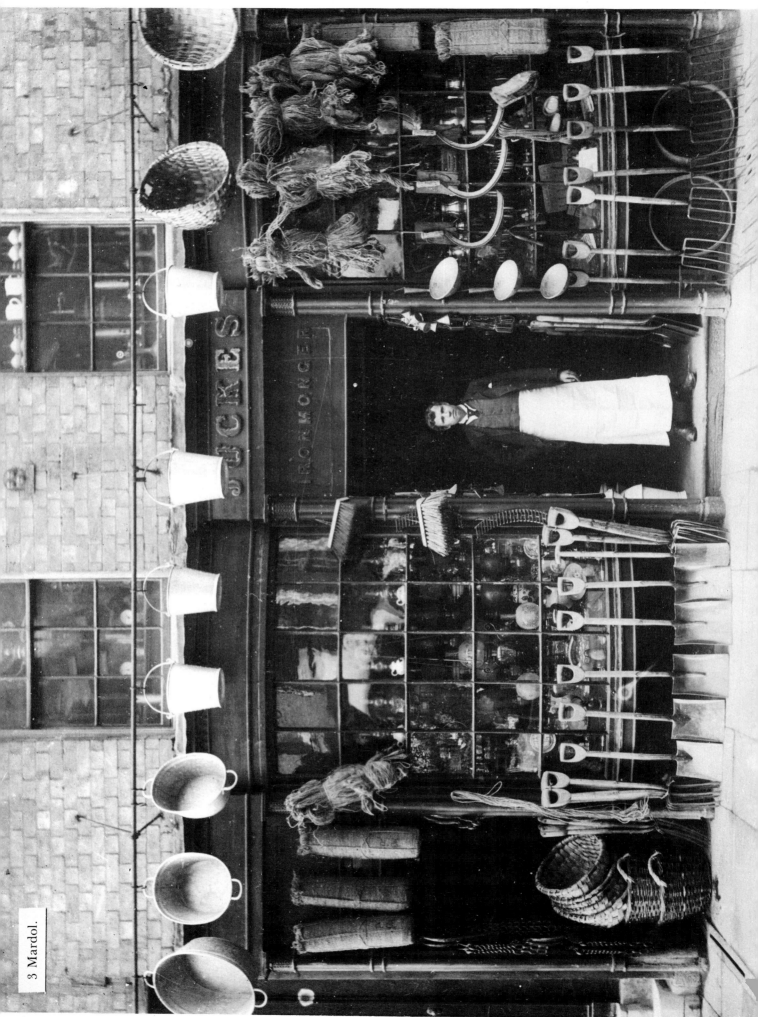

3 Mardol.

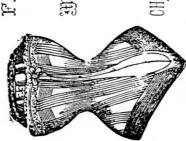

9/10 Mardol.

Edwin Roberts, 25 Mardol.

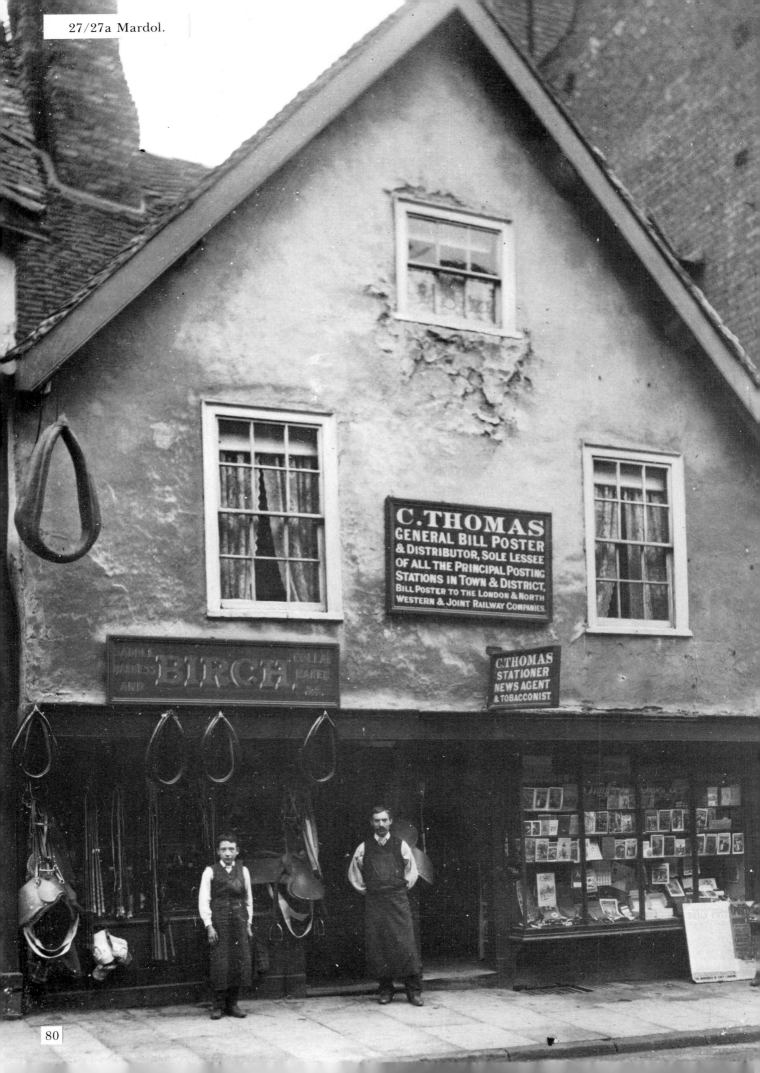

28 Mardol.

29 Mardol.

53 Mardol.

33

THE CANTERBURY
MUTTON Coy.

W. H. SHEPPERD.
CHEAP
PICTURE FRAMING.
MOULDINGS.
CHEAP GLASS.

FOOTBALL
ENGLISH CUP
St. GEORGE'S
SHREWSBURY TOWN
RACECOURSE
On SATURDAY, OCT 13th, 1906

ENGLISH BEEF
— AND —
CANTERBURY MUTTON

1 St. Mary's Street.

St. Mary's Street.

4 St. Mary's Street.

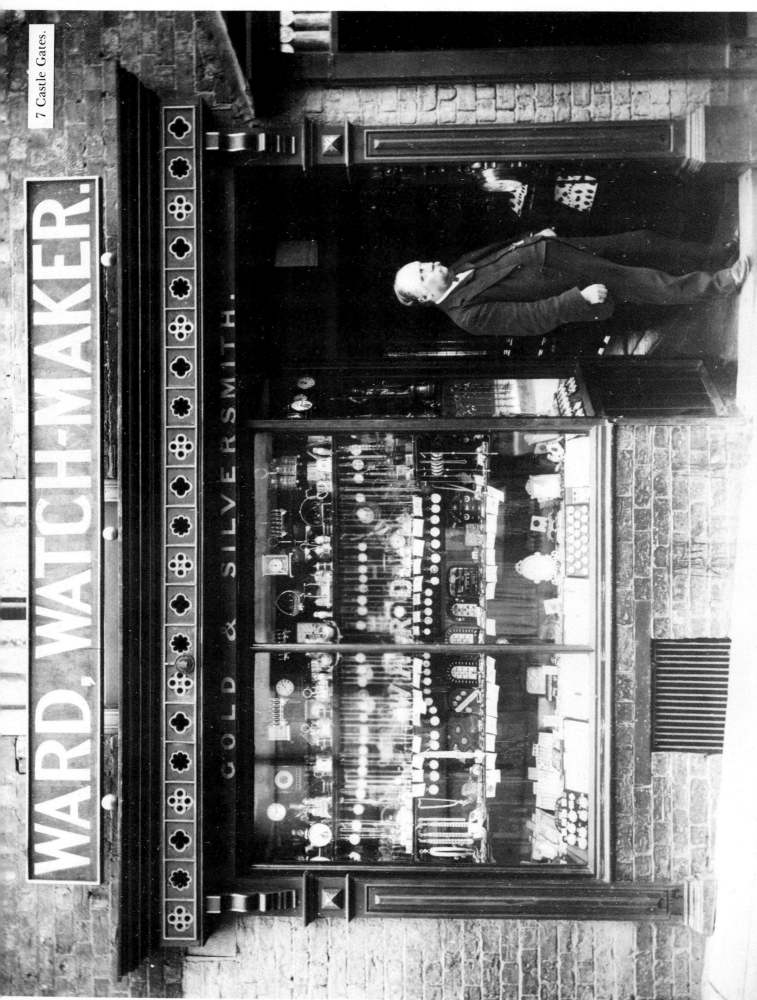

C. Bates, 10 Castle Gates.

91

Henry Hill, 12 Castle Gates.

13 Castle Gates.

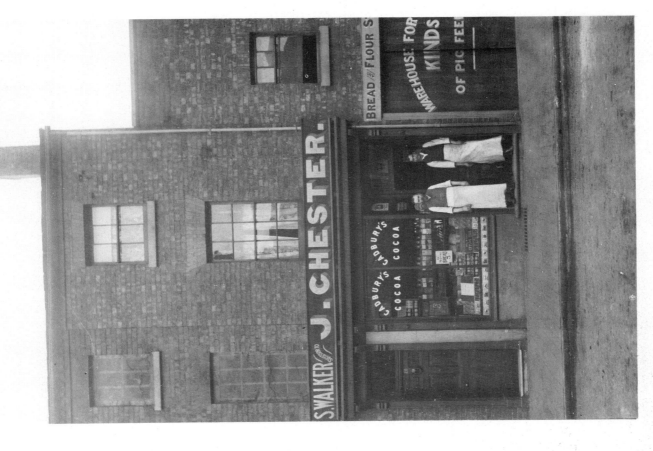

20a Castle Foregate.

MANCHESTER HOUSE.

34.　GUEST.　34.

HOSIER AND DRAPER.

34 Castle Foregate.

86 Castle Foregate.

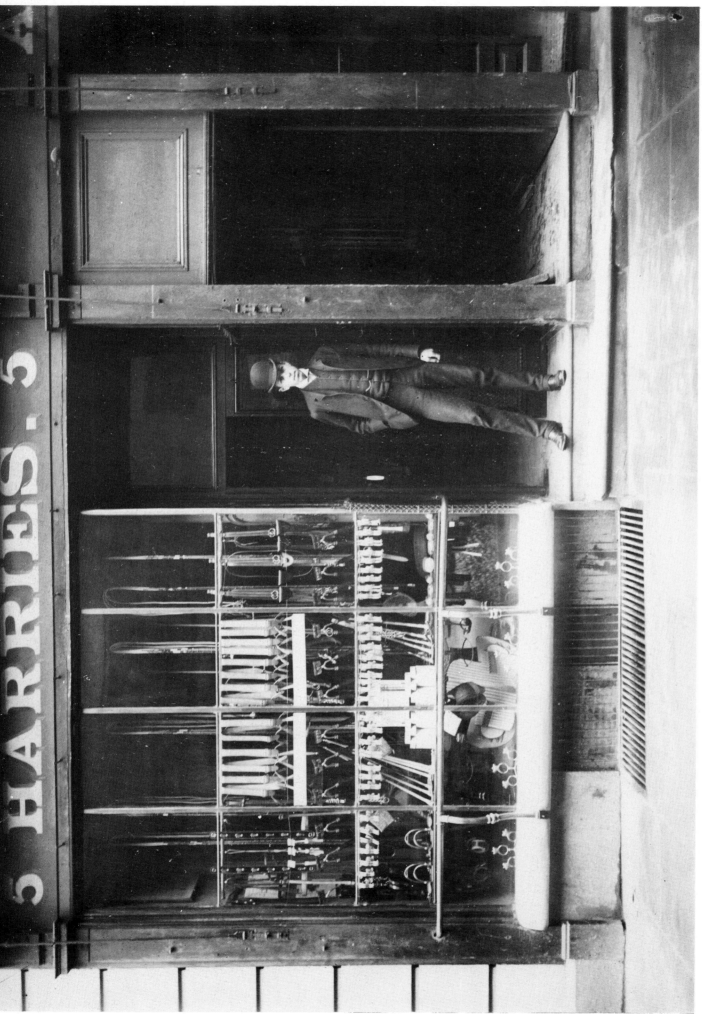

5 High Street.

15 High Street.

Adams, 30 High Street.

Williams, 31 High Street.

45 High Street.

Williams, 14 The Square.

4, The Square.

MR. J. L. DELLA PORTA DEAD.

Notable Business Career.

SHREWSBURY MAN OF VISION AND ABILITY.

Mr. Joseph Lewis Della Porta, head of the well-known Shrewsbury stores of that name, died suddenly on Sunday at his home, Hazlewood, the Mount, Shrewsbury, in his 66th year. He had been ill for about five weeks, and, although he appeared to be recovering, he had a relapse during the week-end.

His father, a descendant of an old Italian family, came to England and started business in Princess Street, Shrewsbury, in 1857. His son, the subject of this notice, was educated at Cotton Hall, Staffordshire, and at St. Omer College, France. At his father's death in 1904, he took control of the steadily growing business. It continued to extend under his enterprise to the larger premises so familiar to Shropshire people. The firm's growth has culminated recently in a large extension with a handsome frontage in High Street. This project was conceived by Mr. Della Porta, and was near to his heart for many years. It is, therefore, particularly sad that death should  intervene a few weeks before the opening of the new premises. He was a model employer, and was held in high regard by his staff.

PUBLIC INTERESTS.

Mr. Della Porta, although deeply interested in a few public bodies, gave his closest attention to his business and his hobby of photography. In the days of its existence, he was a very active member of the old Shropshire Photographic Society, and he acquired the highest skill in this art. He had a most interesting photographic record of Shrewsbury and its surroundings during the changes of the last half century, and competed with great success in local exhibitions. It is believed that he was the first in the town to take up X-ray photography, and, in the early days of its development, did honorary work in that connection for the Royal Salop Infirmary.

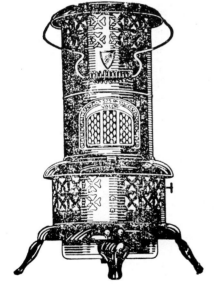

If Father Christmas had Aladdin's Lamp he could hardly command a more wonderful assortment of Toys and Gifts for Children of all ages than is to be seen at ═══

1929

Della Porta's
Shrewsbury

EXCITING TOYS FOR CHILDREN.

HORNBY TRAINS.

HORNBY PULLMAN COACH, Composite. For 2ft. radius rails. Price **11/6**

MILK TRAFFIC VAN. Fitted with sliding door and complete with Milk Cans. Price **3/6**

No. 2 SPECIAL TANK LOCO. Fitted with very powerful Clockwork. Exceptional pulling power. Beautifully finished. Price **22/6**

MINIATURE LUGGAGE and TRUCK. Price **1/6**

No. 1 SPECIAL GOODS SET. One of the latest additions to the Hornby range. Long run and great pulling power. Reversing gear and braking device. Complete Set **30/-**

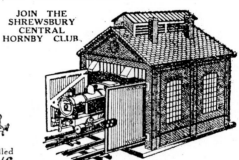

JOIN THE SHREWSBURY CENTRAL HORNBY CLUB.

LUMBER WAGGON No. 2. Fitted with bolster and stanchions for log transport. For 2ft. radius rails. Price **4/-**

TIMBER WAGGON. Enamelled green and red. Suitable for 2ft. radius rails only. Price **3/6**

ENGINE SHED No. 1. This shed is beautifully finished in realistic colours. It will accommodate Locos and Tenders of the M. 0 and 1 types. Price **11/-**

BRITISH MODEL MOTORS, ETC.

BUICK RUNABOUT. A Fine New Model, beautifully finished. Balloon Tyres, Mudguards, Lamps. Price **45/-**

KENT DE LUXE. Chain drive model, Side Doors, Mudguards, Four Lamps, Bulb Horn, Adjustable Seat, Tangent Spoke Wheels. For Kiddies up to 8 years. **49/6**

CHEVROLET DE LUXE. A Fine Car for any Boy. Lamp, Mudguards, and door. Wonderful Value. **29/6**

PEDAL FAIRYKAR. Illustration shows No. 4, a Steel Under Carriage and Forks. enamelled black. Handlebars nickel plated. Price Other styles up to 30/- **10/6**

TIP CARTS. Strongly made and with nicely modelled horses. In Pine from 17/6 down to 5/11. In Elm 28/6 and **22/6**

"UBILDA" AEROPLANES. Set of parts for building an Aeroplane. Makes up into wonderfully strong Model. Price **1/6**

COASTERS. Body made from fine quality Ash, nicely varnished, and Steel Chassis with Disc Wheels and Rubber Tyres. Prices ranging from 27/- down to **7/6**

J. DELLA PORTA & SON,
Princess St., SHREWSBURY.
'Phone 2300.

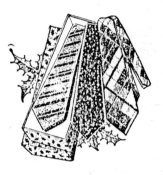

GREEN AND PLEASANT

Shropshire is a county of unsurpassed beauty and interest. "Outer" Shrewsbury, for example Meole Brace, Redhill, Bicton Heath, Gains Park, Bayston Hill, Ditherington and Harlescott, serve as an appetiser for what is to come. To destinations such as Wroxeter, Much Wenlock, Church Stretton, Craven Arms, Bridgnorth, Ellesmere, Ludlow, Clun, Clive, and to all points of the compass, it seems, there is a feast of Shropshire's providing. Shrewsbury itself sets a fine example as the county town.

Boathouse Inn, Frankwell, c. 1880.

The view from Canonbury Bridge, 1895.

English Bridge, c. 1900.

Pengwern Boat Club picnic outing, c. 1910.

Porthill, c. 1907.

St. Chad's Church, 1896.

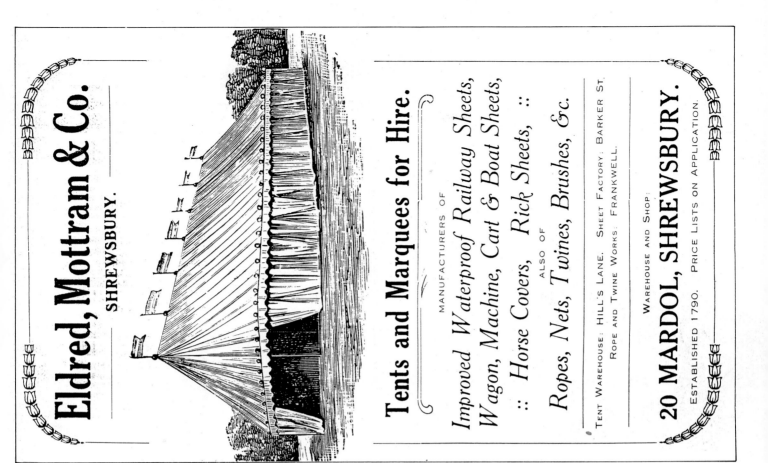

Taking the air. The Quarry, c. 1910.

Sundorne Castle, 1890.

The Dingle, 1923.

ACKNOWLEDGEMENTS

(for providing photographs, for encouragement and numerous other favours)

A.A. Technical Services; Beacon Broadcasting Ltd.; Lord Bernstein; Don Bickerton; British Red Cross Society; Mary and Terry Bullock; Dave Carpenter; Tony Carr; Coleham County School; Anthony Crowe; Fred Dorrell; Girl Guides Association; Clive Hardy; H.M. Prison (Shrewsbury); Anne Jennings; Marjorie Jones; Light Infantry Office, Shropshire and Herefordshire Regiments; Maureen and Colin Michelsohn; Prestfelde Preparatory School; Victor Price; Royal Shrewsbury Hospital; St. John Ambulance; Scout Association; Shrewsbury Cricket Club; Shrewsbury Town Football Club; Shrewsbury Golf Club; Shrewsbury Lancasterian School; Shrewsbury Local Studies Library; Shrewsbury Rugby Club; Shrewsbury School; Shropshire Magazine; Chris Smith; Gordon Stretch; T.S.B. Bank; Bettina Woodall; West Mercia Constabulary; W.R.V.S.

Please forgive any possible omissions. Every effort has been made to include all organisations and individuals involved in the book.